HOW TO DRAW

Barbara Soloff Levy

DOVER PUBLICATIONS, INC.
Mineola, New York

Bibliographical Note

How to Draw is a new work, first published by Dover Publications, Inc., in 2001.

International Standard Book Number

ISBN-13: 978-0-486-47203-4
ISBN-10: 0-486-47203-5

Manufactured in the United States by Courier Corporation
47203506   2015
www.doverpublications.com

Note

If you think you can't draw, or have never tried, follow the steps in this book and you will be drawing right away!

The diagrams, based on simple shapes, show how to draw a pineapple, a house, a sailboat, a cat, a turtle, and much more. The simpler drawings are at the beginning, so it's a good idea to do the pictures in order.

Start with the pear on page 2, and then work your way through the book. You will be erasing the dotted lines on some pictures, so use a pencil, not a pen. You may want to trace the steps of the picture first, just to get a feel for drawing. There's also a Practice Page opposite each drawing page for you to use.

When you have finished your picture, erase the dotted lines. You then can go over the solid lines with a felt-tip pen or colored pencil. Finally, you can color in your drawings with colored pencils or crayons. There are 30 pictures for you to draw, so get started and have fun!

PEAR

Practice Page

APPLE

4

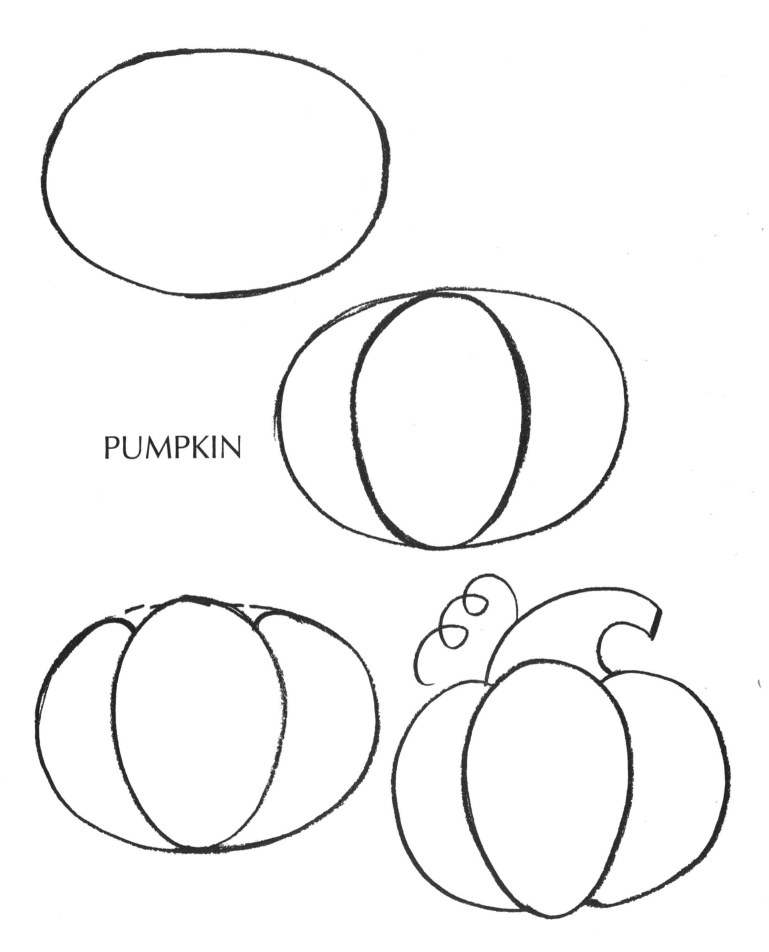

PUMPKIN

PINEAPPLE

8

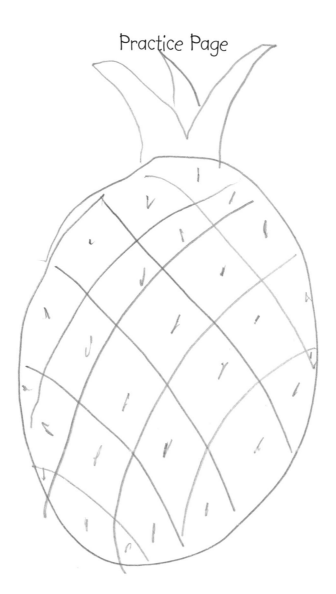

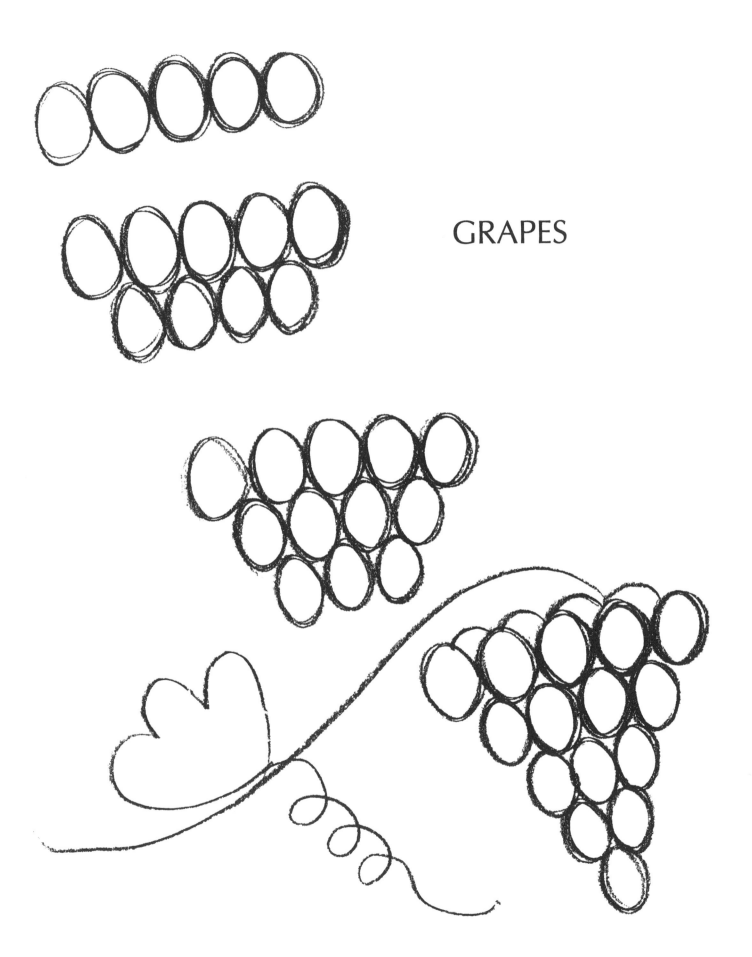

GRAPES

10

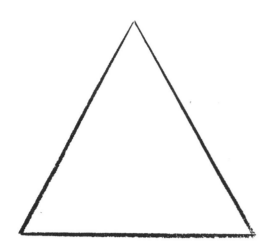

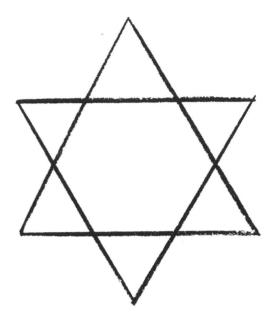

STAR

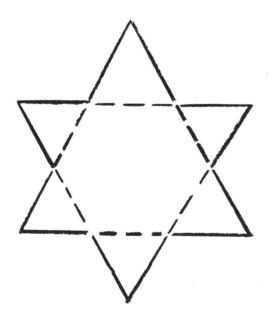

Practice Page

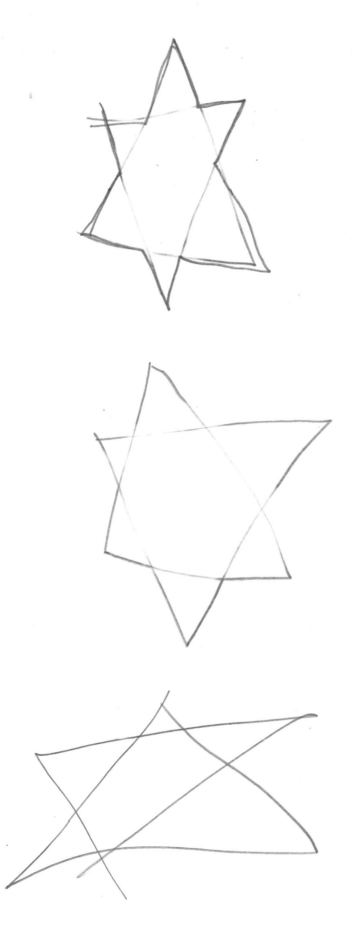

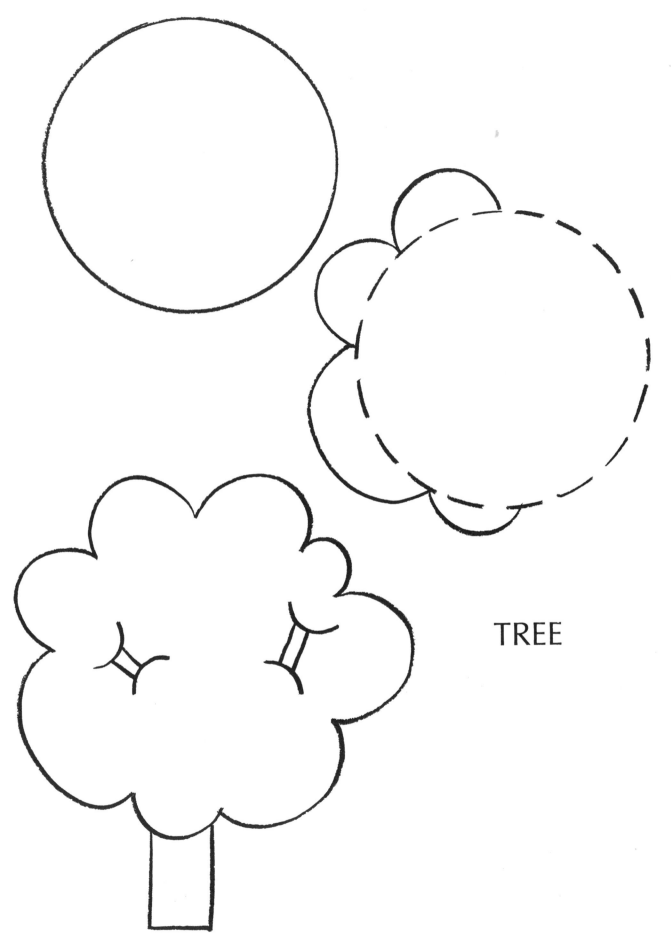

TREE

MOON

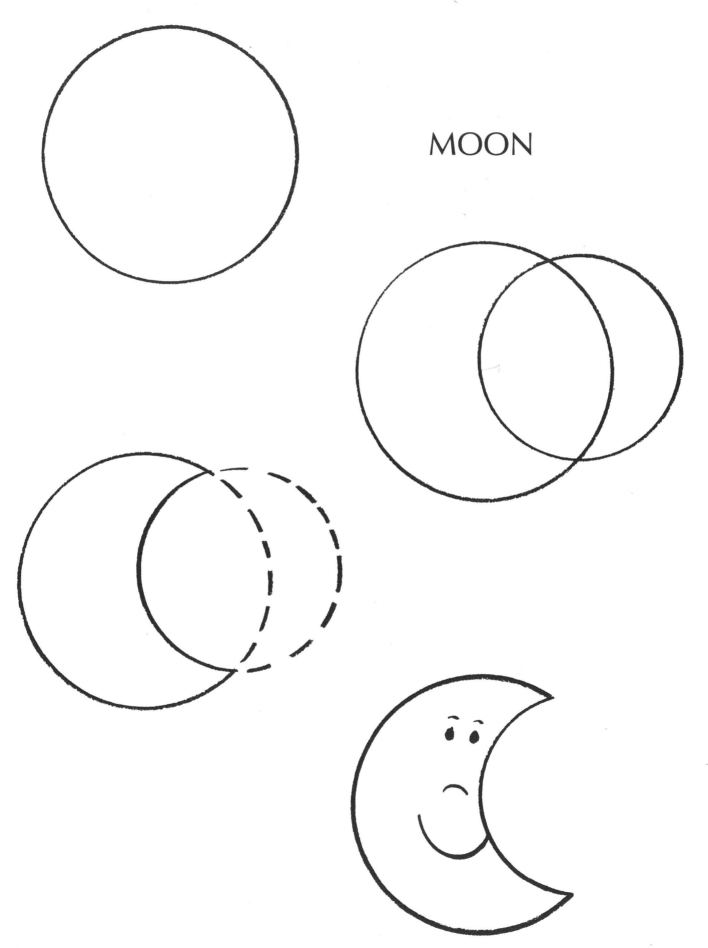

SUN

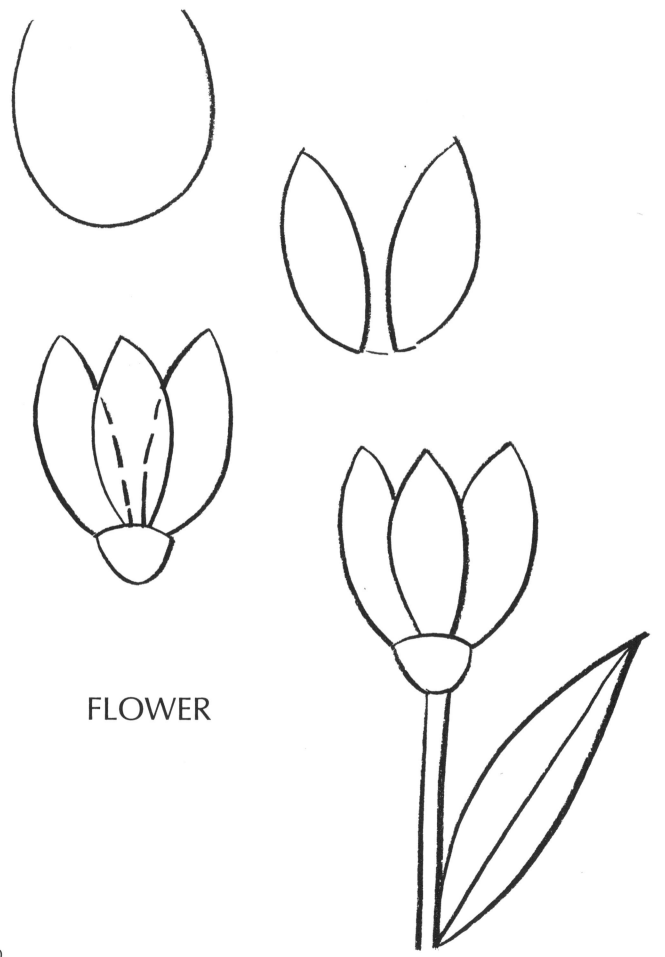

FLOWER

FLOWERPOT
AND FLOWERS

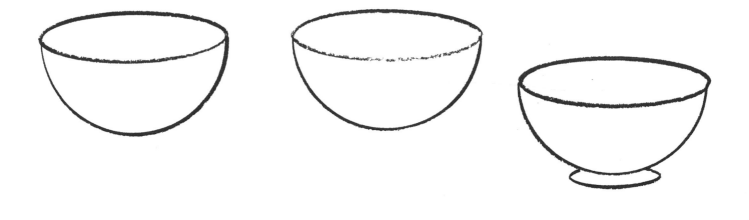

TABLEWARE

24

Practice Page

DOG

Practice Page

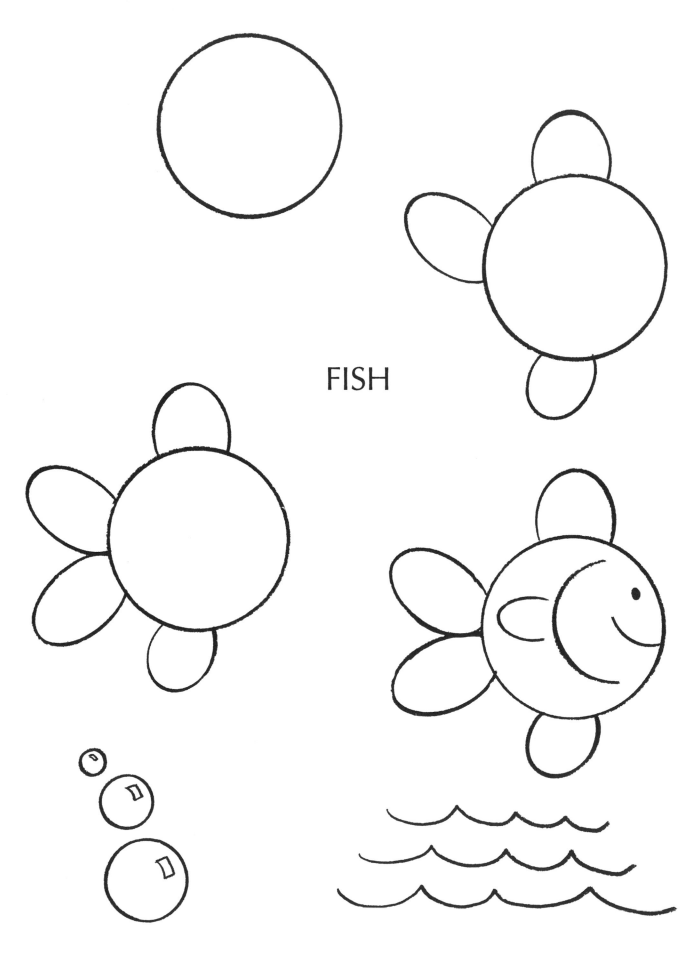

FISH

RABBIT

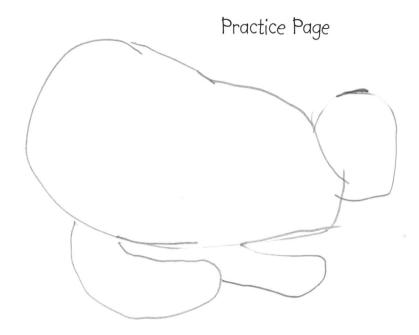

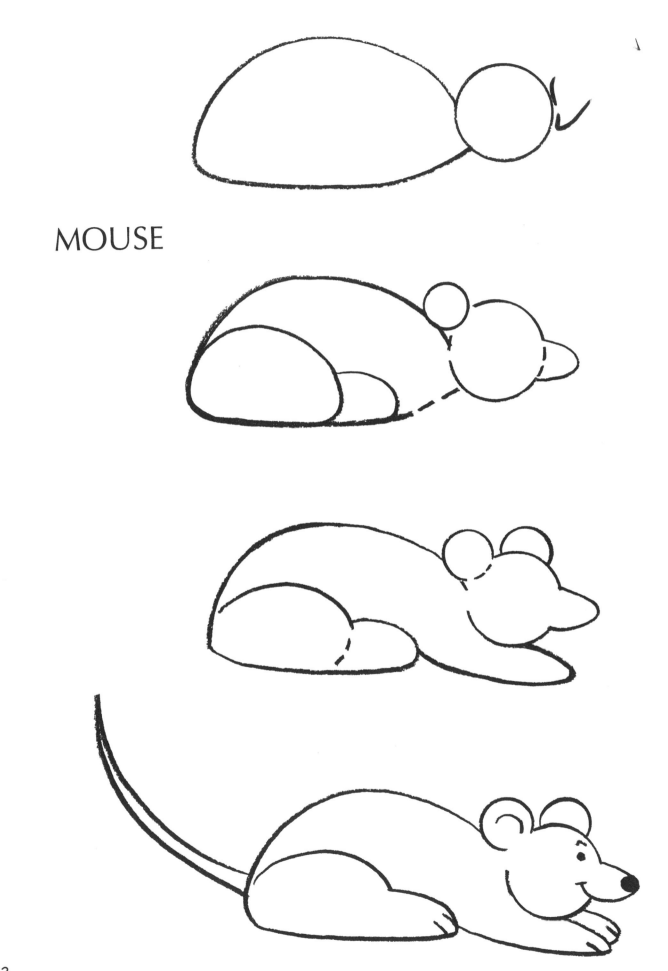

MOUSE

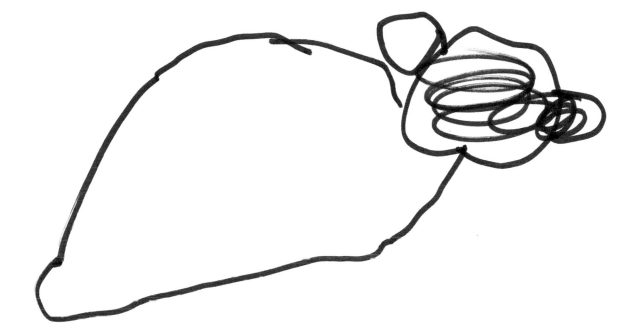

TURTLE

X

FROG

Practice Page

CAT

38

BIRD
AND
HOUSE

40

X

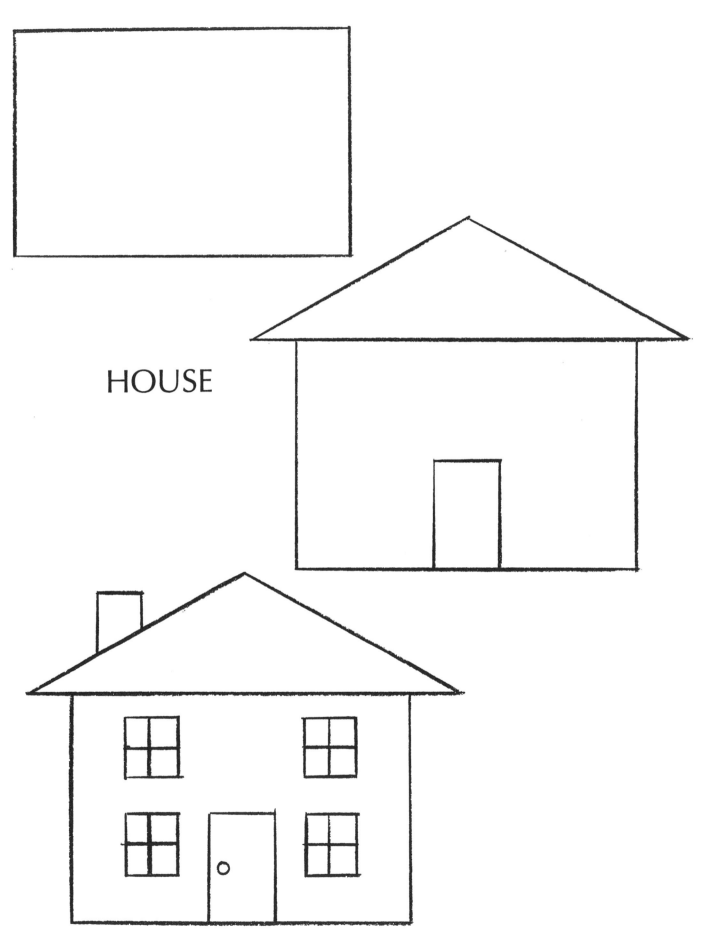

HOUSE

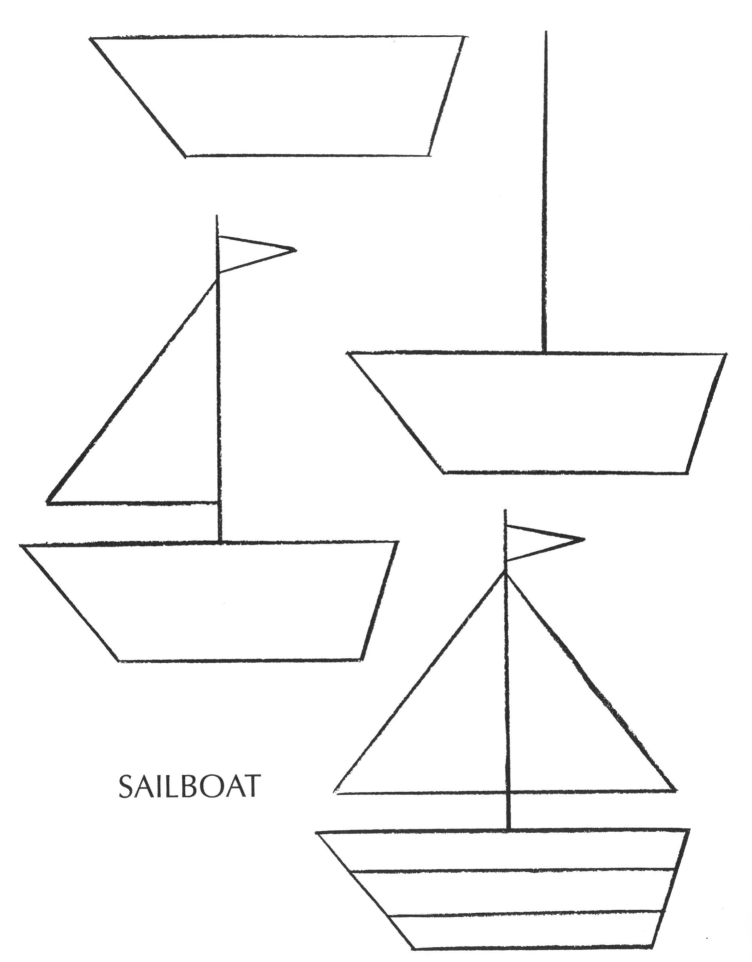

SAILBOAT

Practice Page

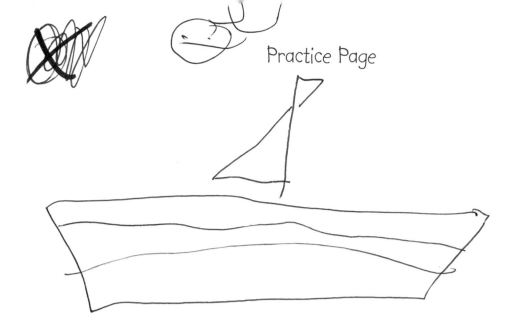

CAR

TRAIN ENGINE CAR

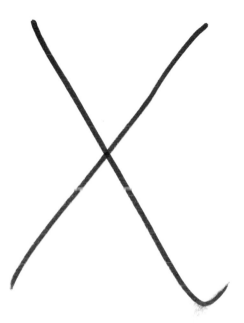

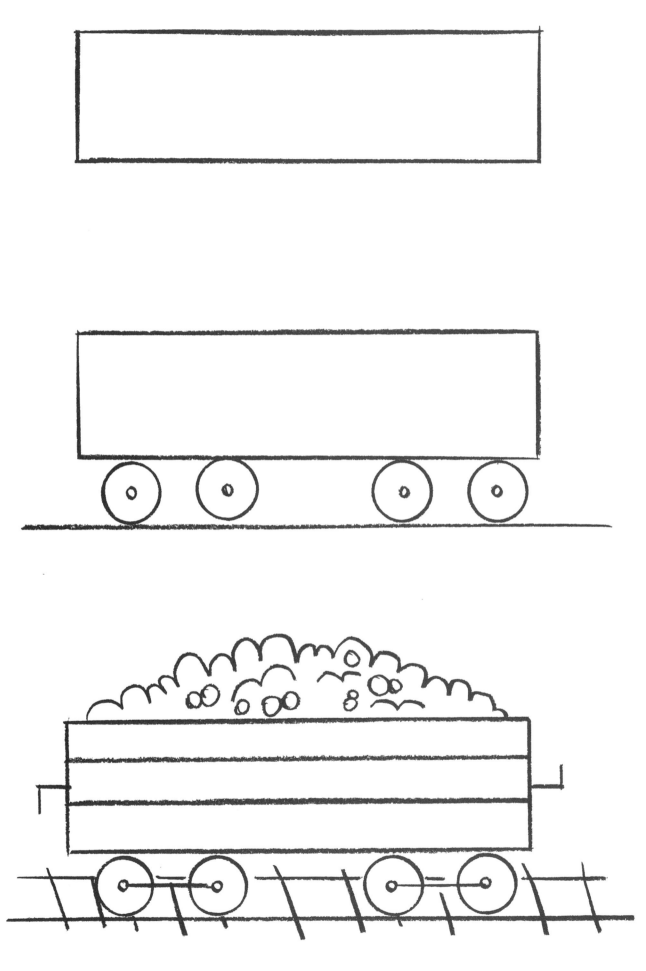

COAL CAR

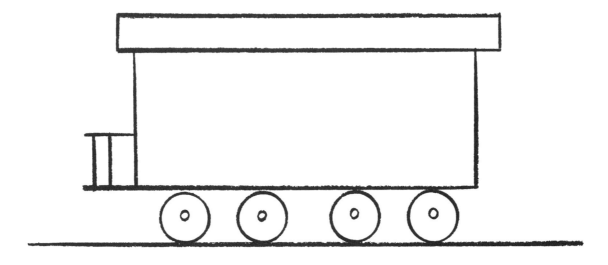

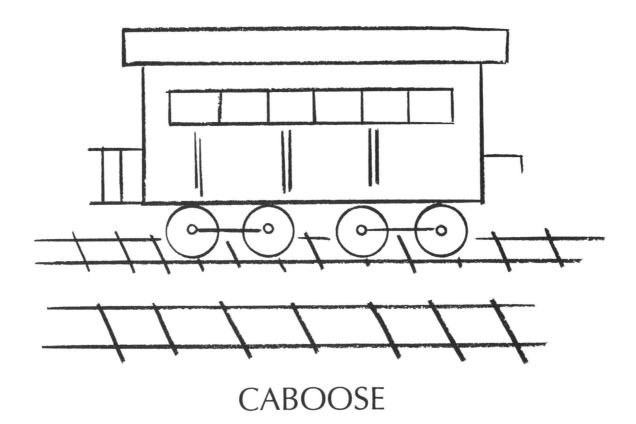

CABOOSE

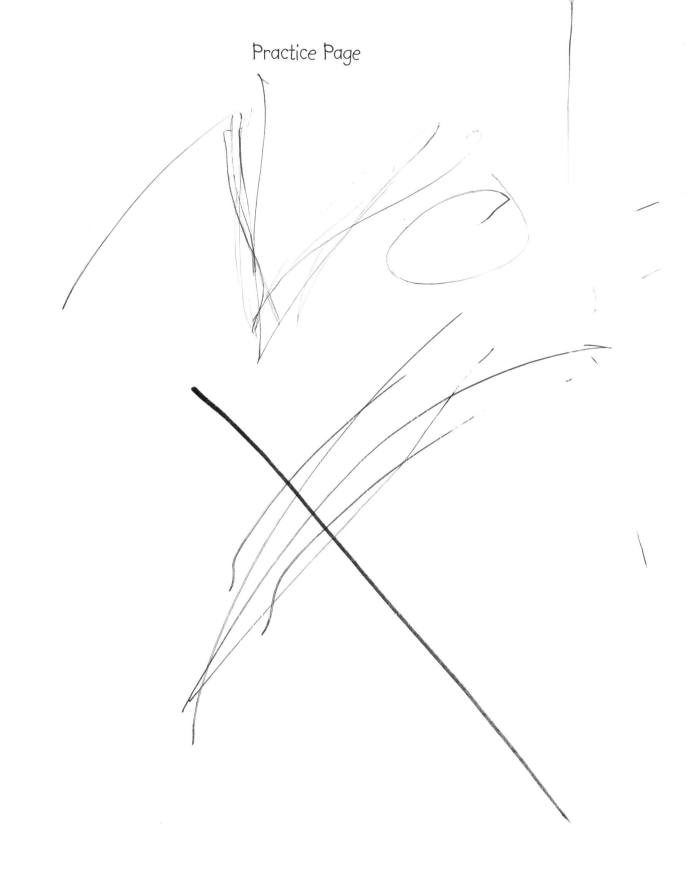

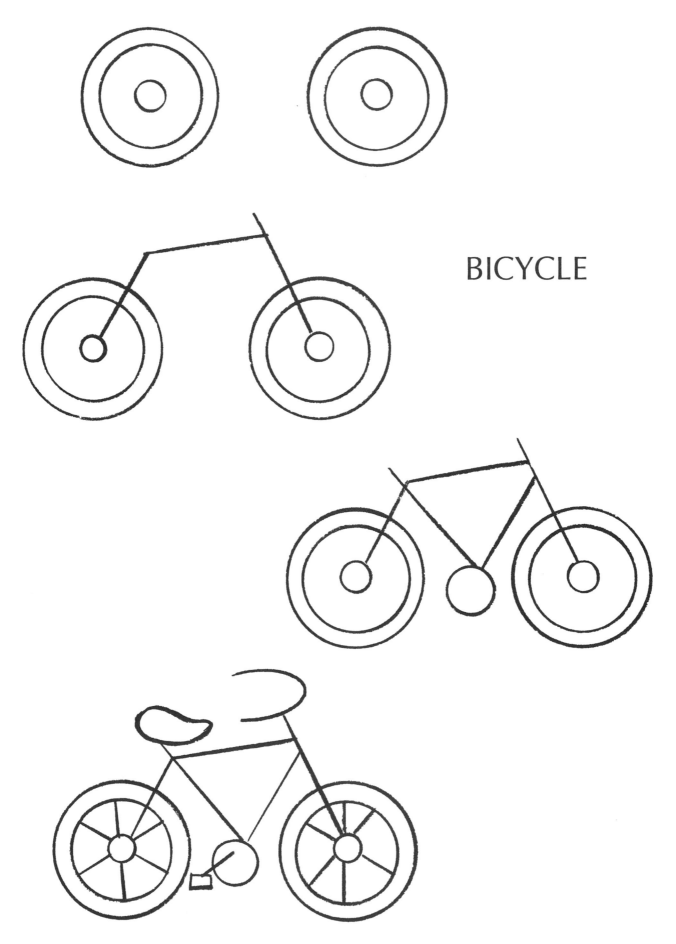

BICYCLE

Practice Page

TRICYCLE

Practice Page

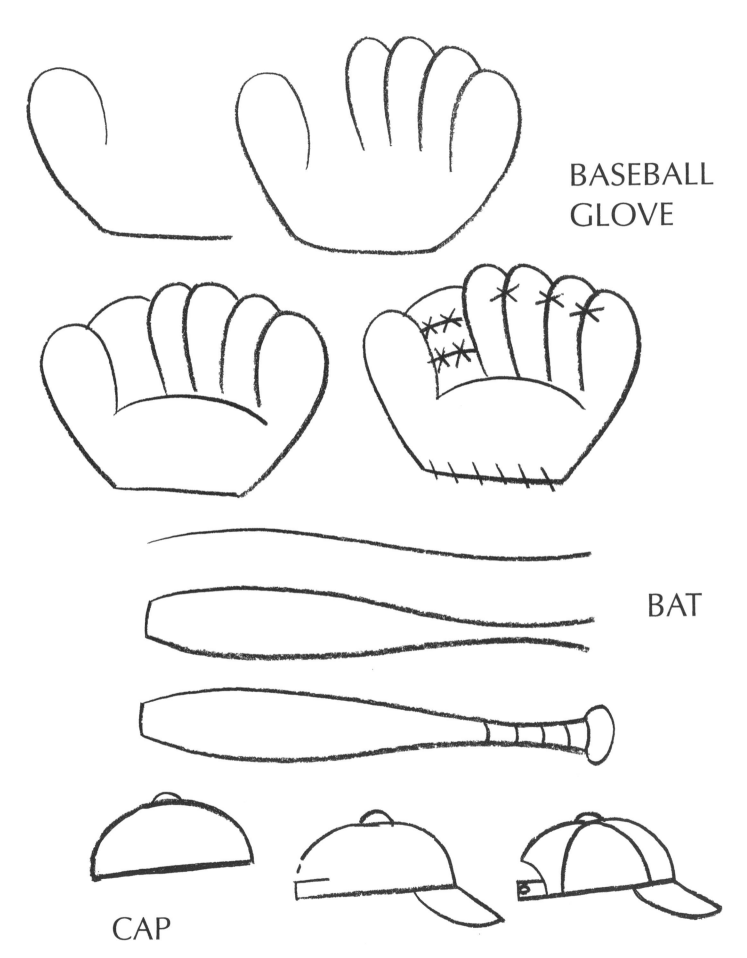

BASEBALL
GLOVE

BAT

CAP

Practice Page

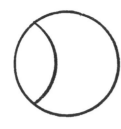

BASEBALL

BASKETBALL

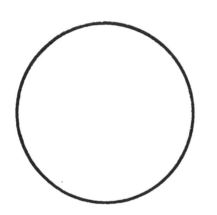

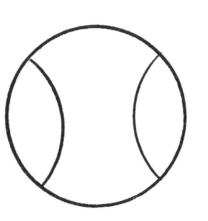

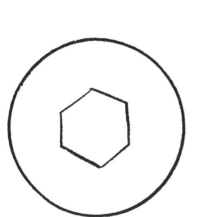

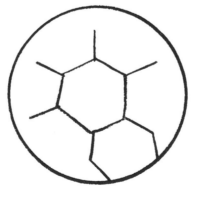

SOCCER BALL